A MOMENT
OF CHRISTMAS
25 December Devotions for Moms

by Anna E. Rendell
foreword by Lisa-Jo Baker

Unless otherwise indicated, all Scripture quotations are taken from the Holy Bible, New Living Translation, copyright © 1996, 2004, 2015 by Tyndale House Foundation. Used by permission of Tyndale House Publishers, Inc., Carol Stream, Illinois 60188. All rights reserved.

Scripture quotations marked NIV are taken from the Holy Bible, New International Version®, NIV®. Copyright © 1973, 1978, 1984, 2011 by Biblica, Inc.™ Used by permission of Zondervan (zondervan.com). All rights reserved worldwide. The "NIV" and "New International Version" are trademarks registered in the United States Patent and Trademark Office by Biblica, Inc.™

Scripture quotations marked CSB have been taken from the Christian Standard Bible®, Copyright © 2017 by Holman Bible Publishers. Used by permission. Christian Standard Bible® and CSB® are federally registered trademarks of Holman Bible Publishers.

ISBN # 978-1-946195-01-2 (first edition)
ISBN # 978-0-578-60630-9 (second edition)

Cover art by Jennifer Tucker, littlehousestudio.net
Interior design by Jared Rendell, jaredrendell.com
Edited by Peggy Johnson and Mary Carver
Author photograph by Jennifer Faris, jenniferfaris.com

Second Edition, November 2019.
Printed in the United States of America

Anna Rendell
P.O. Box 22557
1964 Rahncliff Ct., STE 200
Eagan, MN 55122

AnnaRendell.com

For Jared, Sam, Josie, and Clara –
Christmas is merrier with you.
You remain the best gifts of my life.

TABLE OF CONTENTS

EXTRAS

FOREWORD

The thing about becoming a mother for the first time is how much it changes your body. And how little you expect that. No one warned me about that part. I didn't have a mother to tell me that the pre-baby jeans I brought to the hospital I would absolutely *not* be wearing home.

That memory is what makes Mary so real for me. Because she and I have shared an earthy, bloody experience. She steps off the pages of history for me and into the hard, awkward reality of motherhood because we share a postpartum story.

It's also the reason I stopped singing *Silent Night* the first few years after becoming a mother. I couldn't stomach the words in the light of my new reality - experiencing birth and newborn nights from the inside out - nothing silent about it.

No -- birth in all its awkward, naked, aching reality was much more powerful than that.

It redefined me. And my idea of family and faith.

Because now when I look at my kids, when I look at my adopted siblings, I see in them how much God loves me. How He gave up heaven and Himself for me. How He spread His arms wide to misunderstanding and suffering, to gasps and agony and wanting it to be over and wanting to be released from this calling that cost Him so much.

This salvation, this redemption, this act of bearing children of the new covenant from His body through the mighty act of adoption and delivery on a cross.

We mothers, we get a front row seat at the wonder of Christmas because we've felt it in our weary bones and exhausted souls. How desperately we need peace from all our worries and fears.

And like you, I kneel beside my sleeping kids under Christmas twinkle lights, and I would do it all over again—the uncertainty, the heartache, the labor, the temper tantrums, and the sleep deprivation. Because it's all a gift. The gift of discovering that Jesus loves me this I know, for my children teach me so.

My daughter wants me to climb into bed with her on these cold evenings and she wraps her tiny arms around my head and neck and cradles me close, promising to always love me. We lie by the light of her Hello Kitty lights and I receive the love of a nearly six-year-old. Its weight is all the gold and myrrh and frankincense treasure in the world to me. And as I lie there receiving the unspeakable gift of unconditional love, I feel my tired and weary soul rejoice.

Because Jesus came to love me and wrap His arms around me just like this - all of me. Not just the nice parts. The selfish parts too. The parts He's gently, tenderly rubbing away over years of parenting.

I don't need to perform for Him. I just need to receive.

I'm not always good at remembering that. Especially on the nights I'm snapping at my kids for how they're too loud or too messy or too dirty from all that raking leaves and how they're now traipsing it through my house. There are no silent nights here. But these nights on the princess bed or sofa or out back in the driveway under a basketball hoop or fighting over who gets to use the puppy Christmas wrapping paper are ours. They're our own story and it's a good one, even when it's not a perfect one.

I hope you know that yours is too.

Because there are no advent police.

There are no family traditions enforcers.

There are no report cards given on the kind of memories you're making.

Sometimes doing less is the best gift a tired mom can give her family. Which is why I'm so grateful for Anna's stories. For how she opens her front door and invites us all in so that we can feel that we're OK with our own piles of laundry and imperfect traditions and Christmas cards we forgot to send. Because she reminds us over and over again in a hundred different examples that motherhood isn't about being perfect, it's about being present.

It's OK. You're OK. You're more than OK.

You're knee deep in the sacred footsteps of Mary and her first loud, rough, desperate Christmas. You're there in the muck and the stink and the stable with her. Your kids still rowdy and unpredictable as hers on that first Christmas.

Grace, sisters, grace.

Because after all, it's Him that matters most. And He came to a tired mother with very little flourish, fancy, or perfect.

Love your tiny people, mamas. Crazy ordinary, without expectations love them and that will be more than enough.

From our an anything-but-silent house to yours,

Lisa-Jo Baker
Author of *Surprised by Motherhood, We Saved You a Seat,* and *The Middle Matters,* and co-host of the *Out of the Ordinary Podcast.*

INTRODUCTION

Moms, we are the glue that holds our family together.

We are the ones who create traditions, warm holiday memories, and Instagram-worthy moments. We are the ones who remember all the details: the gifts in their hiding places, the dozen cookies for the preschool party, the clean dresses (and tights, shoes, vests, ties, socks) for Christmas Eve church. We shop 'til we drop for our extended families, choosing just the right gifts for friends and relatives. We stamp envelopes, keep the address book updated, book family pictures, and choose the right outfits to look coordinated (but not too match-y).

At least, we may feel like we're *supposed to* create and do all these things.

So often, we submit to the lure of a Pinterest-worthy holiday, which only lands us in one of two places:

1. Wearing ourselves thin trying to pull off a perfect Christmas: homemade cookies decorated by our perfectly dressed and well-behaved children who would never dream of fighting

over who gets to lick the frosting spoon, an equal number of gifts for each of our children beautifully wrapped and under the tree before Christmas Eve, handmade gifts for the teachers and neighbors and grandmas, a centerpiece involving burlap and tealights on the dining room table, stockings hung by the chimney with care.

2. Or, feeling like a failure. No cinnamon rolls on Christmas morning? Fail. Finding a stack of un-mailed Christmas cards on December 26th? Fail. Having an argument with your husband while burning the midnight oil as you wrestle with packages and assemble toys? Fail. Feeling like you didn't take in as much of the season as you hoped? Fail.

Either we make ourselves sick trying to pull off the perfect holiday, or (most often) we land in the feeling-like-a-failure camp.

When we feel like a failure, guilt creeps in and occupies the space that joy should fill, which often brings on more guilt. It's a vicious cycle, and we pay the price by sacrificing our joy.

As mothers, we can be champions for our children and professionals at neglecting ourselves – especially when it comes to the nourishment of our hearts. We run ourselves ragged making sure our kids have amazing, memorable experiences. We don't sleep enough, we don't feed our bodies well, and we'll feel it deeply, since everything feels bigger and more pronounced during the Christmas season. Beginning with Thanksgiving and lasting through New Year's Day, we set ourselves up for disappointment and guilt as we continually put ourselves in last place.

Friends, this needs to change. Not only do we deserve to be cared for as we care for others, we have to show ourselves this care first.

Have you ever heard the "airplane analogy"? During the announcements given before any flight, the flight attendants remind passengers, "Place an oxygen mask on yourself first before assisting others." We need our own oxygen before we can be of any good to another person. But as mothers, there is nothing we wouldn't do for our kids – including depriving ourselves of that which is life-giving. I think that's why the attendants have to reiterate the process, because it goes against our very nature to care for ourselves first.

And so, this book is for you. The woman being crushed under the weight of Pinterest-pressure. The woman so mentally exhausted she hasn't read anything for herself in months. The woman desperate for connection with her own soul, with others, with Christ. The woman who craves a less-crazed feeling Christmas season, and who longs for a season that is intentional and full of joy.

This devotional was written and designed to offer you a moment of peace, of calm, of Christmas. Toss it into your diaper bag and pull it out while parked and waiting in the preschool pickup line. Reach for this book first thing in the morning before rolling out of bed. Read it while your kids are (supposed to be) napping. Whenever and wherever you decide to take your moment, each devotion is designed to be read in under ten minutes so that it fits right into your very real life.

It's my prayer that, moment by moment, we will make room for the peace and joy that this season is meant to bring. Whether at the beginning of the day before kids and life demand, or at the end of a long day before finally collapsing into bed - whenever you take a moment for yourself, I pray you allow the peace of the season to wash over you.

May our children see us making room for Jesus at our inn, even amidst the to-do list.

May the moments in this book be the guilt-free breaths of oxygen you've needed.

May the stories and thoughts shared within the pages bring you peace instead of pressure, joy instead of guilt, convictions instead of expectations.

And may you have yourself a merry little moment of Christmas.

Anna E. Rendell

Author of *A Moment of Christmas* and *Pumpkin Spice for Your Soul*

DECEMBER 1

The people who walk in darkness
will see a great light. For those who live in a
land of deep darkness, a light will shine.
ISAIAH 9:2

Advent is finally here. The four-week season before Christmas has arrived, and with it a plethora of ways to enjoy it. Advent begins four Sundays before Christmas Day, giving us a built-in way to mark time and count down our days.

It's time to deck the halls, light the pine or cinnamon-scented candles, bake cookies, wrap gifts, and (most of all) celebrate Jesus' birth. The new page on the calendar is crisp and clear, and only just turned over to a new month, beckoning with possibilities.

December days may be some of the shortest, coldest, and darkest of the whole year. . . But they also may be some of the brightest, warmest, and most festive.

Maybe you've recently been in a dark place. Maybe sadness has a grip on your heart, and you're not sure what lightness looks like anymore. These verses from Isaiah bring such comfort in a dark season, promising that though darkness may fill the land, light will shine.

Let's give the light space to do just that: shine bright.

Back to your clean, clear, December calendar page. Before filling it to the brim with activities and tasks and sky-high expectations. . . pause. Take a breath. Think about the list of things you'd like to do this month – all the wonderful traditions and to-dos that are life-giving to you, and to others. Does that list make you smile or make you weary?

Look at that blank calendar again. On December 26th, what do you want to remember about this Christmas season? Which sights, sounds, and feelings do you want your heart and memories to be filled with? Make these the priorities at the top of your list and schedule them in first, because these are the things that bring you joy and light to your days.

What a season it would be if each and every item on our calendar served as a reminder that the darkness has gone, and the light has come. May your December days reflect this truth.

Pray:

Father, thank you for the season of Advent, for a chance to fill my calendar with fun, and for sending Your Son to be the Light in our darkness. Help me to prioritize the month ahead with the things that truly matter – to me, to You, to my family. Amen.

Ponder:

1. Think on the question posed above: on December 26th, what do you want to remember about this Christmas season?
2. How can you shuffle your calendar around to make this happen?

Take a Moment:

Start this season of hustle-and-bustle with your heart in the right place. Start December in prayer.

You wouldn't dream of entering a battle unarmed, or the kitchen without ingredients, right? In the same way, we can't begin the holiday season without a heart open to Him.

Because the only way to stay above water is to trust the One who walked on the waves.

Take a moment to pray. Ask God to calm your heart and bring peace to your weary soul. Thank God for the days ahead and ask Him to help you keep the main things the main things. Your day will feel calmer and fuller, as will your heart.

DECEMBER 2

[Jesus] replied, "What is impossible for people is possible with God."
LUKE 18:27

To kids, some things seem impossible. Remember having that feeling as a kid? Growing up, I recall the impossible:
- Christmas dinners that seemed to go on forever while we waited to open presents,
- Visits to elderly family who asked endless questions and served us 'weird' food, such as pickled beets, sweet pickles, and lutefisk,
- Wearing matching outfits with my siblings that often included not-quite-dry turtlenecks and itchy sweaters,
- Getting up early for Christmas program rehearsals, trips to the mall, and to clean our house before company came.

These situations seemed impossible because all I wanted to do was read my new books, sleep in, wear pajamas, eat the things I liked. . . and as an adult, I realize that all those things were about me. Giving of myself was pretty far from my young and selfish mind. But what I learned from these family obligations (which, at the time, seemed impossible to bear) was that putting the joy of another before our own is a good thing.

Jesus knew this truth and spoke it over His disciples when they had whiny moments. He lived this truth from conception to death. And as moms, we know this to be true because we live it every day for our kids. We put them first to the point where our meals are comprised of scraps from their plates. However, how often do we give our kids the chance to actually experience growth in this area? Yeah, they may whine and protest that it's boring, to which we can offer, "Jesus said that what is impossible for people is possible with God, kids. Ask Him for strength and let's go."

While in context, this verse from Luke speaks to events on a much grander scale, but surely we can speak it over our kids' hearts when fulfilling family (and other proclaimed "boring") obligations. Perhaps not joyful in and of themselves, these events serve as an antidote to selfishness and provide a lovely vessel for learning kindness and true hospitality.

Pray:

Lord, may we not shy away from things we don't like at the expense of another's joy. Help me to provide uncomfortable experiences in kindness for my kids, and to fully participate in them myself. For nothing – even keeping a smile on my face – is impossible with You! Amen.

Ponder:

1. Do you have memories of "impossible" moments from your childhood?

2. What opportunities for uncomfortable kindness can you provide your family and yourself this season?

Take a Moment:

Buy a brand-new notebook (bonus points if it has a Christmas cover), or create a specific Trello board or Evernote for your holiday planning. Make this your go-to space for storing to-do lists, shopping lists, meal plans, ideas for gifts, a ledger of your purchases, etc.

It will streamline your desk and brain to have all those lists in one place, rather than twenty mismatched sticky notes or phone notes strewn about.

DECEMBER 3

In the beginning the Word already existed.
The Word was with God, and the Word was
God. He existed in the beginning with God.
God created everything through him,
and nothing was created except through him.
The Word gave life to everything that was created,
and his life brought light to everyone.
The light shines in the darkness,
and the darkness can never extinguish it.
JOHN 1:1-5

It's happened more times than I care to admit. Inspired and excited, I place my Bible next to my bed and wait until bedtime to read a few verses. The first days go well, and I fall asleep with stories, ancient characters, and Scripture verses dancing through my heart.

But then I get tired. The kids aren't sleeping well, I stayed up late working (or bingeing Netflix), and I skip a night's reading so I can rest a little longer. I vow to renew my reading the next evening, but then. . . you probably know where this is going.

Making the Word a part of my daily practice is often difficult, even though I'm convinced of its importance. I've tried a daily translation of the Bible. Reading plans on my phone. Reading plans printed off. Leaving the Bible open on my kitchen counter. Setting an alarm on my phone. Buying new devotionals and journals. All of this is fun, but doesn't reiterate that the Word comes first, and I'm becoming more convinced that it also needs to come first in my day.

Though these verses in John are referring to Jesus, they apply to the written Word as well. If we make God's Word part of the beginning of our day, our hearts, our life, we'll be plugged into the Source from the start. Like the nightlights in our kids' rooms, it's only when we're plugged in that our light is able to shine. God promises that the Word gives life to all, that His Life gives a Light that cannot be extinguished. This is deeply good news, friends.

Let's set the alarm for a few minutes before our first child will wake. (I mean, let's also be realistic and give ourselves grace when they wake up at the crack of dawn. But even then, let's get that child a book of their own and head down to the Christmas tree to read together.) Let's release ourselves from guilt if we miss a day. Let's plug in to the light that overcomes.

May we begin the days of this Christmas season with the Word.

Pray:
Lord, I love Your Word. Thank you for the chance to read it, to take it in, to share it with my family. Help me to intentionally and consistently make space in my day to plug in to You – first. Amen.

Ponder:
1. What gets in the way of you spending time in God's Word?
2. What little changes can you make to your schedule and heart in order to be plugged into the Bible this season?

Take a Moment:
Prep these caramel rolls at night, before heading to bed. Then in the morning, get up a few minutes earlier than usual. Make a cup of coffee, pop the rolls in the oven, and grab your Bible for a moment of peace. Your family will benefit from both the rolls *and* your peaceful moment!

CHRISTMAS MORNING CARAMEL ROLLS

I make these special caramel rolls for all of our special days. The first day of school, Christmas and Easter mornings, birthdays. . . they're absolutely delicious! I've shared the recipe with countless friends who have now added them to their family traditions as well. It just wouldn't be Christmas morning without them. They pair perfectly with a cup of strong coffee and are very simple to put together. I hope you love them as much as my family does! Makes 16 rolls.

INGREDIENTS:

16 frozen bake-&-serve dinner rolls
1 - 3 ½ oz pkg. butterscotch cook-&-serve pudding mix
½ C. butter, melted
¾ C. brown sugar
1 C. chopped pecans, divided (optional)

INSTRUCTIONS:

1. The night before serving, sprinkle half the pecans in the bottom of a Bundt™ pan that's been sprayed with non-stick cooking spray.
2. Arrange frozen dinner rolls on top of pecans.
3. Sprinkle rolls with pudding mix.
4. Mix brown sugar and butter together; pour over rolls. Scatter remaining

pecans over top.

5. Place pan uncovered in a cold oven and let stand overnight to rise.

6. In the morning, remove pan from the oven and preheat to 325 degrees.

7. Return pan to oven; bake for 35 minutes.

8. Carefully turn pan upside-down onto a large platter. Seriously, be careful – the caramel will be very hot!

DECEMBER 4

*The angel replied, "The Holy Spirit will come upon
you, and the power of the Most High will
overshadow you. So the baby to be born will be
holy, and he will be called the Son of God."*

LUKE 1:35

A couple years ago, my mother gave me
an ornament that read, *God rest ye merry
gentlemen. . . the women are too busy!*

I keep that ornament up all year long, by
my desk. It makes me laugh because it's so
true!

As women, it seems that the joy of the
holidays often falls on us to create. We are
the glue that binds family together,
purchases the perfect gifts and gets them
wrapped, coordinates everyone's activities,
remembers church commitments, writes the
Christmas cards, lights the candles, plans the
meals. . . and the question is: when do we
enjoy *our* silent nights?

We don't want to remove anything from
our to-do lists, and friends, that is okay. The
tasks on our lists are there for a reason, and
it's certainly fine for them to stay. Often,
keeping them on our list means that the
people we love will have a beautiful
Christmas – even as it means we burn our
candle at both ends to make it happen.

But sometimes, it's simply too much.

In addition to the usual holiday
festivities, one of my kids has a birthday in

November, and another has a birthday in December. This adds two more major events to keep track of during an already full season. And one year, my brain and task lists were too full, and it was just too much for me to think about sending Christmas cards.

Now. I've never missed a year of sending cards out. Even when I had both of those babies during the holidays, I managed to send out Christmas cards. Sure, they doubled as birth announcements, and went out after Christmas, but still. I got it done! But that one year, everything was just too full, so I didn't do it. And you know what? I didn't even really miss it. I wasn't upset or disappointed. It freed up both time and money and brain space, and was completely the best choice for me. Then the next year, I sent cards again. No big deal.

With that story, I repeat: what about *our* hearts?

When do we pause to breathe? How do we enjoy this time of Advent? What must we loosen from our grasp so that we may instead grasp the hands that make Christmas what it is – a birthday celebration of the highest importance for a baby born holy? Is it the cards, or the annual open house we host? Is it bringing two dozen homemade cookies to the preschool pageant, or traveling out of state for the holidays?

Whatever your "it" is, it's ok to break tradition in order to maintain your focus. It doesn't mean you'll never do "it" again. But that you can take a break! This is me giving you permission to truly do what works best for you and your family, encouraging us all to keep only the things that matter on our lists, and let go of the rest.

Pray:

Lord, above all I praise You. This is first on my list, and the best way to prioritize – to think on what brings You praise and glory. The rest can fall to the wayside. I love You first, Lord – help me loosen, so that I may grasp. Amen.

Ponder:

1. What, if anything, could you release from your list this year?
2. What little thing(s) will keep until after the holidays?

Take a Moment:

Spend some time with your calendar at the beginning of each week in Advent. Try to plan out as much as you can – meals, shopping trips and lists, kids' activities, church obligations, everything. Use a shared online calendar and add any family events and plans, so you and your partner / spouse are on the same page.

I even go so far as to create a spreadsheet of all the gifts I've purchased throughout the year and how much they cost. This way, at the end of the season, I have a record of what I both gave and spent.

Getting a solid game plan in your head will help keep you feeling organized the whole week – and month!

DECEMBER 5

And because Joseph was a descendant of King David, he had to go to Bethlehem in Judea, David's ancient home. He traveled there from the village of Nazareth in Galilee. He took with him Mary, to whom he was engaged, who was now expecting a child. And while they were there, the time came for her baby to be born. She gave birth to her firstborn son. She wrapped him snugly in strips of cloth and laid him in a manger, because there was no lodging available for them.
LUKE 2:4-7

Let's talk about Mary, the mother of Jesus. She rode a donkey while nearing labor.

Mary *rode a donkey* while nearing *labor*. I didn't even want to get in our car when I was in or near labor; I cannot imagine getting on an animal!

She'd likely been teased and ostracized from her community, after she was terrified by an angel visit that shook her life yet filled her soul.

And when the time came to give birth to this Baby, no doulas assisted, and no nurses fussed. Only Mary's new husband was leaned on, and he filled the roles of doctor, coach, and father. No onesies or tiny diapers were available; rather, simple strips of cloth from who knows where. No nursery to send Jesus to so Mary could rest, just the baleful eyes of donkeys and sheep looked on.

Mary probably cried. I hope she let

herself cry. And I hope she also let herself laugh until she cried again at the sheer bizarre and beautiful wonder of it all. The coming shepherds, the life her Son would live, the angel chorus making the night sky brilliant, a braying donkey the soundtrack, her new husband by her side, and a Baby. Mary's sweet baby boy, born to make her a mama and to make us whole.

And when she'd traveled, birthed, cried and laughed and cried, then Mary praised the One who orchestrated it all.

I often consider Mary at this time of year. Her home wasn't decorated. Her halls weren't decked. Mary's burlap centerpiece lay in a manger – a feeding trough for animals – and her new baby slept in its hold. Immanuel, God with us, delivered by a scared teenage couple in a barn.

It was not a perfect and beautiful scene. Weddings weren't held in that barn; it had never seen a tealight or a mason jar or bleach.

But what it did see, what it did hold, was pure love.

Christmas gives us an opportunity to scrap expectations. The way Christ entered our world was so perfectly imperfect, full to bursting with love and joy, rough around the edges, and so very simple in its appearance. What if we embraced those standards – imperfection, love, joy, simplicity – amidst our to-do tasks and busy season?

Mary didn't expect to become pregnant before she was married. She didn't expect to carry the Savior of the world. She didn't expect to celebrate that first Christmas at all, much less in a borrowed stable.

Yet look at the wonder she welcomed when she threw out her expectations.

We can do the same, me and you. This year, season, week – let good enough truly be enough. Release your heart from the prison of expectations, embrace the hallmarks of that first Christmas (imperfection, love, joy, and simplicity), and it just may be your sweetest Christmas yet.

Pray:
Lord, we praise You. Right here, right now, I lift my heart in praise to You. This busy, messy, wonderful season is all about and for You. You deserve all of our wholehearted praise, and right here, right now, You have mine. May my expectations fly out the window, and may my heart be open to Your leading. Amen.

Ponder:
1. Right in the midst of your chaos, how are you praising the One who orchestrates your all?
2. In what ways can you release yourself from lofty expectations, and embrace whatever God has for you this season?

Take a Moment:
If you don't already have one, Advent calendars are a great way to teach kids about waiting as they count down the days left until Christmas! There are so many varieties of Advent countdowns – there are even

LEGO sets to use as a countdown!

A few of our favorites include classic cardboard boxes with a piece of chocolate behind each window, a Melissa and Doug Countdown to Christmas Wooden Advent Calendar (it's shaped like a Christmas tree, and each day has an ornament with which to decorate the tree), and large coloring pads from the Target dollar section (each day has a new page of activities to color.).

We've also used the Shepherd on the Search from dayspring.com. Each day, you move the Shepherd closer to the manger as he continues on his search for baby Jesus.

You don't need anything fancy, either. Use a classic paper chain, or make an x on a calendar!

However you count down with your kids, first make sure it will work for your family. That's what really matters.

CHRISTMAS REFLECTIONS

_____

_____

_____

_____

_____

_____

_____

_____

_____

_____

_____

_____

_____

_____

_____

_____

DECEMBER 6

Always be full of joy in the Lord. I say it again—
rejoice! Let everyone see that you are considerate
in all you do. Remember, the Lord is coming soon.
Don't worry about anything; instead, pray about
everything. Tell God what you need, and thank
him for all he has done. Then you will experience
God's peace, which exceeds anything we can
understand. His peace will guard your hearts and
minds as you live in Christ Jesus. And now, dear
brothers and sisters, one final thing. Fix your
thoughts on what is true, and honorable, and
right, and pure, and lovely, and admirable. Think
about things that are excellent and
worthy of praise.
PHILLIPIANS 4:4-8

My kids think decorating the Christmas
tree is amazing. They love it, maybe even
more than their mom does (which is saying
a lot). When my kids hang their ornaments,
they end up clumped together at the bottom
of the tree and hanging way down below the
branches. It's not how I would do it, but my
proud children will show off their decorated
branches and play with them until we take
the tree down.

And as to when that actually happens. . .
Let's just say it's well past the twelve days of
Christmas. One year the tree was up so long,
and was so dead, that we actually used a
shovel to scoop up the pine needles. That
fall, I had my third child in four years. I was
so exhausted, and the tree paid the price!

Before having kids, our Christmas tree looked very different. Fragile, shimmering ornaments evenly distributed, presents carefully wrapped and arranged underneath the boughs, and not a single thing made out of Popsicle sticks in sight.

Since having our children, a few of the fragile ornaments have been lost. If the presents make it until Christmas Day unscathed, it's a miracle. Popsicle sticks, macaroni, and glitter are now ever present on the green branches.

It's nowhere near Pinterest-perfect – and it is absolutely wonderful. It brings us all such joy – both the act of decorating and the gift of enjoying our tree for as long as possible!

I used to worry about things like waiting until after Thanksgiving to put up our tree, or getting it decorated perfectly, or using old ornaments that I didn't actually like just because they were sentimental.

Now, I simply choose the things that bring the most joy.

I try to wait until after Halloween to put up the tree. I choose to only hang the ornaments I truly love. I don't worry one bit about what looks perfect, because there are so many more worthy things to think about. I let the kids decorate however they see fit (last year I was taking too long to get the ornaments up, and they started hanging their play kitchen utensils on the tree. I got the message and picked up the pace.). All of this brings me and my family soul-deep, heart-swelling joy.

When we pause to actually consider all that God has given us, it can take our breath away.

Joy lives in the spirit of the giver, not in the presentation of the gift.

I love what our tree now looks like, in all of its mismatched, sweet, simple, low-branch-clumped beauty. It's real life glory up there, and that is worthy of praise.

Pray:

Help me, Lord, to embrace Popsicle stick perfection. Nothing in my life belongs on Pinterest, and right now that's a good thing because my children are watching me live real. Help me to see Your glory reflected in my joyful mess. Amen.

Ponder:

1. What areas of your Christmas celebrations are less than perfect? Why do they bother you?
2. How could you embrace them?

Take a Moment:

Set up a small artificial tree in your kids' bedroom! Let them decorate it as they wish, using their own special ornaments. My sons' tree includes colored lights and miniature ornaments that he loves; my daughters' tree is pink! We turn their trees on before bed, so they serve as a nightlight.

The kids look forward to this all year! And besides their joy, it's an easy way to give them meaningful ownership of our family celebrations.

DECEMBER 7

How precious are your thoughts about me, O God.
They cannot be numbered! I can't even count
them; they outnumber the grains of sand!
PSALM 139:17-18

We know what our kids love about Christmas. We can rattle off their favorite traditions and events without a second thought:

"She loves baking with me, flour coating the
counter and floor and ceiling. He loves to watch
holiday movies, snuggled in on the couch and
cuddled under blankets. She wants to go looking
at huge Christmas light displays. They all stay
awake in their beds on Christmas Eve, sleepily
listening for sleigh bells. And if we don't make
frosted Christmas cookies, heaven help us."

We know everything about our kids when they're little. We can name the silly, sweet, big, and small things that matter most to their hearts. But how about you, mom? What are *your* favorite things about the Christmas season? What matters to your heart? Because those things have weight and importance, and they belong on your to-do list right alongside the Christmas cards and grocery shopping.

You matter.

In the Psalms, we're told that God thinks of us more than there are grains of sand. Isn't that incredible?

In college I worked at a Bible camp as a

counselor, spending week after week with cabins full of teenage girls. Those were the best summers of my life. Each night I would lead our cabin in a devotion, something experiential that would help the truth of God sink deep into our hearts. One of my favorite devotions was to walk down to the beach, read those verses from Psalms, and tell the girls to lick one of their fingertips and stick it in the sand.

I know. It's weird. Stay with me.

They'd hold up their sand-covered finger, and I'd ask them to count the grains of sand on their fingertip. Of course, they couldn't. Then I'd ask them to imagine sand covering their whole hand. Next I drew their attention to the lakeshore we sat on, and then the sand at the bottom of the lake in front of us. There are more than 10,000 lakes just here in Minnesota, you know, and then we'd take lakes in other states into consideration... finally the ocean beaches, and the actual sand at the bottom of the sea.

All of those grains of sand, and God thinks of you more.

If you're being crushed under the weight of everyone's needs, if your Christmas-ing has been put on the back burner for years, and if it's all because you think that's where it all belongs . . . think again.

You matter. You are thought of, a *lot*, by the Creator. He designed you with a unique personality and is not at all surprised by the ways in which you love to celebrate His birthday because, like you with your kids, He knows you deeply.

If you need a few hours alone in front of the tree to relax and refresh, ask your spouse or a grandparent to take the kids out shopping, then sit yourself to that chair by the tree without an ounce of guilt. If you love baking sugar-sparkled goodies, make a batch of dough for the kids to play with or decorate while you mix up an old favorite of your own. If decorating the house makes your heart pitter-pat, deck those halls early in the season, and maybe while the kids are asleep. Read a favorite Christmas book in the evenings. Spritz on a delicious holiday fragrance that you just love. Blow-dry your hair on a Tuesday, just because!

Build in time for the things that make you say, "NOW it feels like Christmas!" You deserve to have the Christmas glow just like the people you take care of, because Christmas is not just for kids.

Jesus was born for you, too.

Pray:

Lord, I am grateful that I matter to You. Thank you for the reminder that I am just as important as my kids are, and that it is okay to make space for the things I love to our holiday traditions. Amen.

Ponder:

1. During this season, what are the traditions and activities that are most special to your heart?
2. How can shuffle around your schedule to make room for the things that feed your soul?

Take a Moment:

As you deck the halls of your home, be intentional about the décor you set out. Do you really, truly love it? If not, place it in a separate bin. At the end of the season, donate whatever items are in that bin.

Your home will be a little lighter and only decorated with the things you treasure, and who knows? Your lovely pieces may become the treasures of another family!

DECEMBER 8

She gave birth to her firstborn son. She wrapped him snugly in strips of cloth and laid him in a manger, because there was no lodging available for them.
LUKE 2:7

I am a perfectionist. I can't even say I'm a recovering perfectionist, because if I'm really honest I know I haven't completely given up those tendencies. I want things to be lovely and pretty close to perfect, and at times I've sacrificed the happiness of my family to obtain it. I've snapped at my husband, dressed my kids in cute, matching outfits instead of what they chose, and stretched myself way too thin in the name of making perfect memories. I give up sleep and patience, and even kindness flies out the window in hopes of getting things perfect.

Quite a contrast to the hearts behind the very first Christmas.

When I read about the birth of Jesus, I can't help but think of the births of my three kids. In a hospital, in a clean and sterile room, nurses caring for us. If I needed medical attention, I got it. If I was hungry, someone brought me food. I was able to bathe my new babies, wrap them in new cozy fleece sleepers, and rest them in a bassinet while I snoozed in a soft bed. It was quiet and safe and warm, and a pretty perfect way to welcome life into the world.

That first Christmas was less than

perfect, yet it was glorious. It was the greatest mix of holy and human. There was straw, animal smell, and a star. There were expectant hearts, new parents, and kings.

At the start of the season, we have a choice to make. We choose to chase perfection, or we choose to chase holy.

When they are grown, what will make our kids nostalgic about their Christmases past? Let's make those the things that take center stage in our holiday celebrations. Our kids won't remember being late to church, a burned cookie debacle, or if the bathroom floor was clean. Our kids won't remember perfect days. They will remember the warmth of their home, the traditions we started together, and most of all, they'll remember how we made them feel.

This year let's drop perfect. Let's chase holy instead.

Pray:

Father, help me in this often stressful season to be patient, to remember that my family and friends will remember how I made them feel. Help me shepherd their feelings and focus on the things that matter. Grant me patience and joy so I may make my family feel special and cozy and loved by me. Grant me the openness to feel the same way by You. Amen.

Ponder:
1. What areas of perfection are you willing to drop?
2. What do you think you could gain if things are less than perfect?

Take a Moment:

Let your kids help. . . for real. Give them jobs that matter. Let them sign the Christmas cards, cut out the cookie dough, set the table, or hang the breakable ornaments on the tree.

Will it take longer? Maybe. Will it be worth it? Absolutely. They will feel your trust and give you the gift of their imperfection and love.

DECEMBER 9

Long ago the LORD said to Israel: "I have loved you, my people, with an everlasting love. With unfailing love I have drawn you to myself."
JEREMIAH 31:3

Has it been one of *those* days? Are you feeling defeated, defensive, alone? Have you said something you regret? Are the kids running wild? And is it only 9:00 am?

Take a breath.

You need to know that you – yes, you – are doing a fantastic job. There is no other time of year that may make us feel more inadequate, pressed for time, impatient, and comparison-filled than Christmas. Isn't that sad? I'm pretty sure that's not what God had in mind when a lowly stable was filled with His glory, housed in a baby.

So today, however much is left of it, know deep down that you are enough because God in you is enough. Your Christmas is enough – for your kids and your family – because of the love you have poured into it. And at the end of the day, if the "only" things you've accomplished are having kept the kids out of the presents, fed them and yourself, and given a bunch of hugs, then, mama -- you did it. It was enough. And you are loved unfailingly.

Pray:

Lord, fill me with Your patience, love and joy today, because I do not have these things on my own. Stay with me as I try to parent well and cram more into this day than is actually possible, and help me to do it with grace. Give me the peace that passes understanding, and when my head hits the pillow tonight, assure me that today I have been enough because You are. Amen.

Ponder:
1. When you're having one of those days, what small things can you do to get it back on track?
2. How can you help your kids get back on track with you?

Take a Moment:
Do you have a collection of Christmas CD's? Keep them all in one case! That way, when you're heading out of the house, you can just grab the case and be on your way with some Christmas cheer in hand.

If you don't have CD's anymore, create a Christmas-only playlist on Spotify or iTunes. Pull it up on your phone and sing along! If you need inspiration, I've created a great playlist for you; find it at bit.ly/amocplaylist.

DECEMBER 10

For everything there is a season,
a time for every activity under heaven.
A time to be born and a time to die.
A time to plant and a time to harvest.
A time to kill and a time to heal.
A time to tear down and a time to build up.
A time to cry and a time to laugh.
A time to grieve and a time to dance.
A time to scatter stones and a time to gather
stones.
A time to embrace and a time to turn away.
A time to search and a time to quit searching.
A time to keep and a time to throw away.
A time to tear and a time to mend.
A time to be quiet and a time to speak.
A time to love and a time to hate.
A time for war and a time for peace.
Ecclesiastes 3:1-8

For some, Christmas can be a time of anguish and pain. Missing family members no longer with us, bearing the marks of infertility, financial problems, and so on. All this and more can hamper the supposed joy of the season that we're "supposed" to feel.

Thank goodness for these verses, and for our old friend Charlie Brown. They both show us that there's room in the holidays for emotions besides joy.

Remember in *A Charlie Brown Christmas* when sweet Charlie confesses to his friend, Linus, that he just isn't feeling the Christmas spirit?

Charlie thoughtfully says, "I think there must be something wrong with me, Linus. Christmas is coming, but I'm not happy. I don't feel the way I'm supposed to feel."

Or how about when he visits his mailbox, finding it empty again? Charlie says, "Rats. Nobody sent me a Christmas card today. I almost wish there weren't a holiday season. I know nobody likes me. Why do we have to have a holiday season to emphasize it?"

We can all relate to our old pal Charlie, and we can all find a piece of ourselves in his story. We can have high expectations of our holiday feelings thinking, *"It's Christmas! We are supposed to be rejoicing and feeling all the warm fuzzies! We are supposed to set the tone for joy!"*

But sometimes we simply aren't able to do this. There is no guilt in feeling your very real, very valid, emotions.

There is a time for all of it.

As these verses in scripture say, there is a time for each and every emotion we experience and feel. Often some of the feelings listed in these verses crop up two at a time. Sometimes they take turns or trade off, one for the other. And instead of burying it, these passages encourage us to feel it all. To lean right into the pain, if need be. These verses make space for it all.

God welcomes our honesty. He wants us to bring Him the nitty-gritty of our feelings, the raw emotions we often suppress because He sees us. He sees the pain and fears you've been hanging on to, and He beckons welcome.

There is no supposed to. There is only Him, and He invites your all, right into Christmas.

Pray:

God, You know my struggle. You know my pain. I want to be happy, but Lord. . . I'm not sure how I'm supposed to feel. So I bring it all to You. I place this pain, this unknown and confusion, in Your hands, and I ask for Your healing to be bigger than my despair. I love You, and I trust You with this. Amen.

Ponder:

1. What pain are you harboring this year?
2. Are you able to bring it to the Lord? Why or why not?

Take a Moment:

Scent can be a path of comfort to our heart. It can set a peaceful tone for our home, making it a welcoming space. And it can really just make it feel like Christmas!

Make a batch of this super simple Holiday Stovetop Simmer to bring holiday scent into your home, without any toxins or chemicals. Better yet, double the recipe and gift it to a friend! She'll be touched by your thoughtfulness.

HOLIDAY STOVETOP SIMMER

I first made these simmers with a group of crafting friends from church. We each made two bags – one to keep, one to gift. It was such a simple and enjoyable time together!

INGREDIENTS:

One orange, quartered (leave whole if gifting)
½ C. fresh cranberries
1 Tbs. whole cloves
3 whole cinnamon sticks
1 tsp. grated nutmeg
1 bay leaf

INSTRUCTIONS:

1. Place ingredients in a small saucepan.
2. Add water until ingredients are covered.
3. Simmer on low heat, refilling water as it evaporates.

If preparing to give as a gift, place all ingredients in a paper bag. Tuck a copy of these instructions inside:

Quarter the orange. Place all ingredients in a small saucepan filled with water. Simmer on low, refilling water as needed. Breathe deeply, and have yourself a peaceful moment of Christmas.

CHRISTMAS REFLECTIONS

_____

_____

_____

_____

_____

_____

_____

_____

_____

_____

_____

_____

_____

_____

_____

_____

DECEMBER 11

*So the Word became human and made his home
among us. He was full of unfailing love and
faithfulness. And we have seen his glory, the glory
of the Father's one and only Son.*
John 1:14

*Silent night, holy night,
all is calm, all is bright. . .*
Doesn't a silent night sound fabulous?!

Our schedules are already full, and the
Christmas season adds to the chaos. Parties
to attend, gatherings to host, volunteering at
school, special services at church, traditions
to uphold, dinners to plan. . . the list goes on.
And it's a good list! Full of family, friends,
and fun. All lifegiving. All wonderful. All-
consuming of space on your calendar and in
your mind.

Speaking of your own list, where do you
fall? Are you even on it? If at all, I bet you're
toward the bottom, and we all know what
happens to the bottom of our lists. They're
the first to be left undone, un-crossed off,
carried over to the next day, week, or
month.

If you're not high up on your own list,
the season is going to overtake you like a
strong current. Has it already? Are you going
under? Right now, stop. Just take one
moment to breathe. For real – breathe,
slowly, deeply, in and out. Remember the
airplane analogy – *put on your oxygen mask
before assisting others*? This is the time to do

that. Get that oxygen mask on so you will be able to do all that you want to do to help your family experience the joy of this season!

What will help you breathe deep enough to take in the God turned Man, born for me and for you and for us all? The great thing is that it doesn't have to be a weekend retreat in the snowy mountains. Since Jesus has made His home among us, He is all around. We can see His face, His glory, in the faces of our loved ones. In the reflection of a clean bathroom mirror. In the quiet of a hearthside movie after the kids are in bed. Glimpses of glory all mingled into our everyday moments.

I think that's just how He likes it.

Mom, get thee a silent night, and take a moment to steep in wonder.

Pray:

Holy Father, this season. . . it is miraculous indeed, and so is Your love. We are celebrating this wondrous thing that happened thousands of years ago, yet Your love for me is as strong now as it was then. May I slow down enough, even just for a moment, to embrace that love and peace. Amen.

Ponder:
1. Where do you see glimpses of God's glory?
2. What can you intentionally work into your busy schedule to make sure you're refreshing your heart?

Take a Moment:

Actively plan for a quiet night after the kids are in bed – even though it's late and there are projects to check off. You deserve to give yourself a gift of time. So mark your calendar and keep this appointment!

Make a cup of hot cocoa or tea. Light the room only by the Christmas tree lights and maybe a favorite scented candle, and curl up under a quilt.

Use these few quiet moments to breathe, slow and deep, and reflect on what this season of miracles means to you.

DECEMBER 12

. . .the Lord himself will give you the sign. Look!
The virgin will conceive a child! She will give birth
to a son and will call him Immanuel (which means
"God is with us.")
ISAIAH 7:14

We're asked to believe a lot when we believe in the Christmas story. From prophecies long foretold coming true, a virgin conception, a barnyard birth. . . the whole thing is something only a big, loving God could've orchestrated and carried out.

God asks us to believe, just as He asked people long ago to believe. He asked the main players in the Christmas story to do incredibly difficult things, to witness miracles, to believe the actual impossible, and then He delivered.

Elizabeth and Zechariah, a wizened couple, were asked to believe that they could still bear children in their old age.

Mary, an unwed teenager, was asked to believe the impossible about her own body.

The Magi, miles and years away from meeting the child Savior, were asked to believe their prayers would be answered.

Joseph, betrothed to a woman carrying Someone else's child, was asked to believe that everything would be ok.

Not only did God ask them all to believe, but He asked them to believe in *good things*. Sometimes those are the hardest things to trust, because we fear what may happen if the other shoe drops. God asked the people in the Christmas story to believe in His goodness, to buy into the good, and to make their fear smaller than their belief.

God is asking us to believe the same today.

No matter what we're facing this season, this day – this moment! – we can believe and trust that God is good, and that He will do good in our life.

Pray:
God, help my unbelief. Where You are working for good in my life, help me embrace it more than I embrace the fear of the flip side. Help me trust in the impossible good that comes from You. Amen.

Ponder:
1. What impossibility are you facing?
2. What impossible good is He asking you to believe?

Take a Moment:
Dinner feeling impossible? Spend a day in your kitchen prepping freezer meals for busy December days! Just a few hours can turn out several meals. Your freezer will be stocked, your budget will be on track, and your family will thank you because they'll be full of a delicious meal – and you won't be stressed about what to make. Win win.

DECEMBER 13

For a child is born to us, a son is given to us. The government will rest on his shoulders. And he will be called: Wonderful Counselor, Mighty God, Everlasting Father, Prince of Peace.
ISAIAH 9:6

Jesus, the King who came to save the world, was once a child with a mother. Isn't that an amazing thought? I often wonder how He was as a child. Inquisitive? A little mischievous, maybe? Quiet and observant, taking everything in through a lens that none of us possess? We won't know this side of heaven, but I love thinking about who Jesus was as a child.

I also have a lot of questions about, and for, His mother.

How was it to raise the Savior? How was it to both mother in ordinary ways – dishes, cooking, cleaning, caring, holding, pushing, encouraging, clothing, teaching – and extraordinary, soul-stretching ways? I can't even imagine the ways in which Mary had to multitask her heart for this job of raising Jesus to be both man and God.

Talk about being all things to all people.

Though our lives are incredibly different, every mother can still relate to Mary. Who of us have not tried to be all things to all people?

One difference is that we are not made to be all things – both in big and small ways.

As moms, we are not all Instagram-worthy decorators, top chefs, and amazing bakers. We do not all love to make Pinterest crafts with our kids. We do not all excel at shopping for the perfect gift, serving on the church committee, and entertaining family & friends over a meal. We may be gifted in one or more of these areas, but no one is fabulous at them all.

We are not all things, especially at Christmas. When I try to be all things in one day – working mom, stay-at-home mom, great cook, creative kid-entertainer, art director, shopper extraordinaire – I am a wreck by noon. We cannot be all things to all people. We can't even be all things to our kids, our spouses, or to ourselves.

The good news? There is One who can be all things! Jesus is a Wonderful Counselor, Mighty God, Everlasting Father, Prince of Peace.

Only Jesus, the one who came to make a mother and save the world, is all things. Only Him. Not us. This is truly good news.

Pray:

Jesus, thank You. Thank You for being so, so much more than me. Thank You for filling all these roles and more. Help me lay at your feet the roles I don't need to fill. Amen.

Ponder:
1. What roles do you try to force yourself to take on when you don't feel equipped and/or don't enjoy them?
2. How can you let go of these roles?

Take a Moment:

This foolproof fudge recipe is just that. It's super easy and super delicious. Make and wrap up a batch to gift a friend, teacher, neighbor, or your own family.

FOOLPROOF MICROWAVE FUDGE

I've made this fudge for years and it never lets me down! I like to add different toppings to each batch, then mix & match in a clear gift bag for a sweet present.

INGREDIENTS:
3 c. high quality semisweet chocolate chips
1 – 14 oz. can sweetened condensed milk
1 tsp. vanilla extract
Toppings (optional): crushed candy canes, mini M&M's™, marshmallows, pretzels, sprinkles, etc.

INSTRUCTIONS:
1. Line an 8x8 pan with wax paper. Let the edge of the paper hang over each side of the pan – this makes it easy to lift out after the fudge is cooled.
2. Spray the paper-lined pan with non-stick cooking spray.
3. In a large glass bowl, combine chocolate chips and sweetened condensed milk. Microwave on high for 2 minutes, then slowly stir in vanilla until the mixture is smooth.
4. Pour mixture into prepared pan.
5. If you're adding toppings, press them gently into the top of the fudge now.
6. Let cool on the countertop until

mostly firm, then lift out wax paper, and cut fudge into squares.

7. Let cool completely before packaging up.

DECEMBER 14

*And the one sitting on the throne said, "Look, I am
making everything new!"*
REVELATION 21:5

There are years when celebrations seem
thin, pale, even trite. Years when, for
whatever reason, we find ourselves going
through the motions, unable to really
experience or take it all in. Years when, what
used to make celebrating sweet, now seem
overdone and fake.

What's a mom to do when traditions get
stale, celebrations get old, and our hearts just
aren't in it?

Take a breather. Sit down. Center your
heart. And ask God to make new what is old.

Start with recalling the ancient story. A
stable scene, set long ago, with a cruel king
and angel choruses, sheep and shepherds,
Magi en route and a new mama smitten with
her Son. There were no traditions for her
family yet, as the Reason to celebrate had
just arrived. They didn't hop on Facebook to
see what all the other families were doing to
celebrate. No, they simply soaked up their
own brand-new family, quietly reveling in
what the Lord was up to.

There is so much we can learn from that
first Christmas when we reframe it as
something new. They say Scripture is the
living Word of God; this means there's
always something new we can learn from
the old stories. What a gift.

When you need a breath of fresh Christmas air, when all the usual ways you celebrate and recognize the holiday seem timeworn and uninspired, when it seems things have been said and done many times, many ways... take a moment and recall the One who makes all things new.

He's willing and waiting to breathe new life into your heart today.

Pray:
God, I need a breath of fresh air in my soul. Things are feeling flat and forced, and I want them to be renewed and full. Breathe Your spirit into my heart today, Lord, and into the heart of our celebrations. From Your place on the throne, make both my heart and holidays new. Amen.

Ponder:
1. What traditions feel worn out?
2. What would it take to make them feel new again?

Take a Moment:
Have a cookie swap with friends! It's easier than you may think. Bake or buy two dozen cookies (or bars, or dipped pretzels, or whatever deliciousness you like.). Invite friends to bring their own treats to contribute and set the goodies out around your table. Take 2-3 of each cookie until they are evenly distributed to all attendees.

Everyone goes home with about two dozen different cookies – not too many, not too few, and all new to you! Easy as that.

DECEMBER 15

*An angel of the Lord appeared to them, and the
glory of the Lord shone around them, and they
were terrified. But the angel said to them, "Do not
be afraid. I bring you good news that will cause
great joy for all the people. Today in the town of
David a Savior has been born to you; he is the
Messiah, the Lord. This will be a sign to you: You
will find a baby wrapped in cloths and lying in a
manger." Suddenly a great company of the
heavenly host appeared with the angel, praising
God and saying, "Glory to God in the highest
heaven, and on earth peace to those on whom his
favor rests."*
LUKE 2:9-14 (NIV)

The shepherds. Mary. Joseph. The wise
men. Even the innkeeper.

Mingled into the wondrous beauty of the
Christmas story, there are those who
experienced fear of it. Mary and Joseph,
fearful and wondering, were reassured by
angels. The Magi made the wise yet fearful
choice to flee from Herod's orders,
continuing their travel along a different
path. The innkeeper was asked for a room,
yet had to turn away a woman in labor –
and if that didn't strike fear into his heart, I
don't what would!

And these precious shepherds. Can you
imagine? Being in the quiet countryside,
nearing sleep, their sheep tucked in for the
night. The campfires burning embers,
stoked just enough to keep warm. The

dishes were done, the work completed for the day, and all was still. Then suddenly, throngs of angels, singing and shining! Not just glowing like the star at the top of your tree – no, it was the unfiltered glory of the Lord that shone in Technicolor! Gone was the stillness, and their first reaction was fear.

Not that I blame them, or anyone else who was afraid of God and His messengers, because sometimes the things God asks us to do are terrifying. The things He asked of these people were huge, life-altering, enormous asks.

Yet they all said yes.

Each and every one of them obeyed, despite their fears. That's huge, because we can do the same thing. When God calls us out of our comfort zone, we can obey and step out in faith. When God asks us to do something scary because people might look at us like we're different, we can obey and stare straight ahead at Him. When God shows us another path that may look less traveled and less secure but maybe, just maybe, there's a better life around the corner. We can walk on boldly.

Our fear can lead to our obedience.

One comfort found in fearful obedience is that our fear of God is good – healthy, even. He is *God*, after all! We don't have to fear Him in a traditional sort of way (He has promised to bring us good and not harm) but rather in more of an awestruck, wonder-filled, overwhelmed by glory, kind of manner. In each of these parts of the first Christmas, we can see that, despite their fear, the people who heard God's call and obeyed were deeply blessed by the outcome.

God is good, even when we are afraid.

Pray:

Lord, sometimes Your glory scares us. Sometimes seeing Your glory in ourselves and in others scares us. But we know You are good, and we know you're doing good in us. May our hearts be beautifully fearful of You. Amen.

Ponder:

1. What is something you feel God is asking of you that is frightening, but good?
2. How can you take a baby step in obedience?

Take a Moment:

Count down the last few days until Christmas with an old-school paper chain. Easy and fun for kids to put together, you could even add an activity, prayer or hope on each daily link. Remove one link before bed each night until Christmas Day!

CHRISTMAS REFLECTIONS

DECEMBER 16

"That is why I tell you not to worry about everyday life—whether you have enough food and drink, or enough clothes to wear. Isn't life more than food, and your body more than clothing? Look at the birds. They don't plant or harvest or store food in barns, for your heavenly Father feeds them. And aren't you far more valuable to him than they are? Can all your worries add a single moment to your life?

"And why worry about your clothing? Look at the lilies of the field and how they grow. They don't work or make their clothing, yet Solomon in all his glory was not dressed as beautifully as they are. And if God cares so wonderfully for wildflowers that are here today and thrown into the fire tomorrow, he will certainly care for you. Why do you have so little faith?

"So don't worry about these things, saying, 'What will we eat? What will we drink? What will we wear?' These things dominate the thoughts of unbelievers, but your heavenly Father already knows all your needs. Seek the Kingdom of God above all else, and live righteously, and he will give you everything you need. So don't worry about tomorrow, for tomorrow will bring its own worries. Today's trouble is enough for today."

MATTHEW 6:25-34

Sometimes when I'm really happy and enjoying life, I worry that the other shoe is going to drop. If there's not chaos somewhere in my days, I almost feel guilty and I definitely feel worried. I find myself inviting stress into my formerly peaceful heart, opening the door to pessimism, and welcoming in the worry and what if's. What kind of living is that?

There is no guilt in enjoying your days, in loving your life, in celebrating the little moments that may actually be the big ones.

In these verses from Matthew, Jesus is teaching. He's teaching His disciples, He's teaching people that randomly showed up, and He's teaching people who'd been waiting to hear a word from Him. Jesus is teaching and I think we need to pay attention to what He's saying. This is a big chunk of scripture and it's one that can change our very lives and legacies.

Jesus tells us that we don't have to worry. We don't have to worry about our basics, like food and drink and clothing. God will provide for us as He does the birds and fields.

But maybe you've been in a place where you did worry where your next meal would come from, or about how you were going to afford shoes for your kids, or about how your ends would meet. Did it happen? Did it work out? Did God use someone to pay a bill, buy the shoes, or give assistance that came at just the right time for you? I earnestly hope so.

These verses don't let us off the hook in terms of caring for one another; rather, they invite us to be the answer to someone's prayer. Like both the birds and the lilies who sometimes need care in order to survive, sometimes we need to be cared for too, in big and small ways.

When you're in a place to do so, pay for the meal. Give to the cause. Drop the "mom nod" to a mom covered in kids in the grocery checkout lane. Send a card in the mail. Pay the tab. Donate new clothing instead of used. Sponsor a family's Christmas.

Help ease the burden of tomorrow's trouble that someone is secretly carrying and in doing so, let your heart be light.

Take in this day of Advent, this day of big and little things, of delights and disappointments, of highs and lows. Make an intentional decision to let your heart be light, and to have a merry little Christmas indeed.

Pray:

Lord, You tell us to not worry about anything, whether big or small. I want to enjoy this season in all its complex simplicity, and I want to have a light heart that's full of joy. Help me let go of the heaviness I'm carrying, and – even just for today – live light and merry. Give me the courage to be the answer a prayer for someone when I'm in the position to help them. Amen.

Ponder:

1. Why is it almost easier to gravitate to a heavy heart than a light one?
2. How can you be the answer to someone's prayer this week?

Take a Moment:

Clean out your closets! Gather the things that are in great shape but that you and your family no longer absolutely love (items that no longer fit your body or purpose), and donate them. Allow yourself only a small pile of clothing that is in the "someday I may wear this again" category. Begin the New Year lighter, simplified, and blessing others.

DECEMBER 17

"Blessed is she who has believed that the Lord would fulfill what he has spoken to her!" And Mary said: "My soul praises the greatness of the Lord, and my spirit rejoices in God my Savior, because he has looked with favor on the humble condition of his servant."
Luke 1:45-48 CSB

I struggle with "not fair-itis." You know – the feeling that creeps in when someone else gets an opportunity I'd like to have, or even feel that I deserve? Or when their family appears more put together than the three-ring circus I have at home? Or when she fits into her pre-baby jeans at three days postpartum and I still don't fit into mine three years after giving birth?

The last thing I feel in these situations is peace.

All the main characters in the Christmas story could absolutely have had similar feelings of "not fair- itis."

Joseph was engaged to a girl who was pregnant, and not with his child. Not fair!

Mary was pregnant and living out a plan far beyond her control, and also had to travel while nearing labor. She was away from home when she delivered her new baby. Not fair!

Elizabeth, Mary's cousin, had tried for years to conceive and was unable to do so. I myself have been in that place of infertility, where everywhere I turned I saw pregnant women. Not fair!

Yet God was pleased with each one of them. Scripture says each of them "found favor with Him," and it shares some of their emotions with us – including Mary's joy and song of praise.

Mary rejoices in the unfair love of the Lord.

You read that right. It's absolutely unfair how deeply God loves us, that He is pleased with us, and that we are constantly in God's love no matter our circumstances. Many people throughout Scripture, including the ones in the Christmas story, experienced the unfair gifts of God.

Elizabeth became pregnant in her old age. Unfairly wonderful.

The shepherds got a glimpse of heaven. Unfairly glorious.

And Mary sings praise to the greatness of the Lord after finding out that despite her purity, she would give birth out of wedlock. Yet she praised God. Unfair devotion, in and of itself a gift from Him.

When you find yourself slipping into a fit of unfair-itis, remember how God loves us in spite of, because of, and no matter what – just like He did the people in the Christmas story. And though we may not understand our circumstances, we can try and respond as Mary did, with thanks and praise and trust in the One who ordains our days.

Pray:

Lord, Your love is so big – big enough to cover my petty thoughts of fairness. Help me to obey and love like Mary, despite the unfair feelings of the situation. Everything about You and Your grace is unfair in the very best way. Amen.

Ponder:

1. What things trigger feelings of unfairness in your heart?
2. How can you head them off, choosing a peaceful heart instead?

Take a Moment:

Make an entire night out of going to pick out the perfect Christmas tree - whether your tree lot is in the grocery store parking lot or the middle of a forest. Bring travel mugs of hot cocoa or cider, crank up the Christmas tunes, and take your time choosing just the right tree.

Even if the kids melt down, have to go potty in the middle of the woods, or spill the cocoa, you'll make plenty of sweet real-life memories!

DECEMBER 18

This is how Jesus the Messiah was born. His mother, Mary, was engaged to be married to Joseph. But before the marriage took place, while she was still a virgin, she became pregnant through the power of the Holy Spirit. Joseph, her fiancé, was a righteous man and did not want to disgrace her publicly, so he decided to break the engagement quietly.

As he considered this, an angel of the Lord appeared to him in a dream. "Joseph, son of David," the angel said, "do not be afraid to take Mary as your wife. For the child within her was conceived by the Holy Spirit. And she will have a son, and you are to name him Jesus, for he will save his people from their sins."

All of this occurred to fulfill the Lord's message through his prophet: "Look! The virgin will conceive a child! She will give birth to a son, and they will call him Immanuel, which means 'God is with us.'" When Joseph woke up, he did as the angel of the Lord commanded and took Mary as his wife.
MATTHEW 1:18-24

The Christmas story is one of holy obedience.

If just one player in this grand story had decided to go their own way, reply, "No" to the call, or ignored the sound of that still, small voice, it wouldn't be the story we know and cherish. God would surely have found a way (God always finds a way), but if our hearts are soft to His first idea, things seem to go more smoothly.

It's like we tell our kids – ninety-seven times a day – to please listen the first time we ask. We know that they would skip over hurt, pain, misunderstanding, and mistakes, if they would just listen and obey right away. How often do they decide to go their own way, say "no!", or ignore our voice?

How often do we?

Like we do for our kids, God sees the bigger picture. He knows the plan for our lives and can see 100 different outcomes at once. And if we follow His lead before our own, things usually work out for the better.

God used the first-time obedience of Mary and Joseph, the shepherds, the Magi, and even the innkeeper to carry out His holy plan. The wonderful and wondrous thing is that God still uses our obedience today.

What incredible things could God accomplish in our lives, hearts and families if we gave Him a "yes" the first time He called?

Pray:

Lord, I want to hear You clearly and not delay in my yes. Your plans for our life are glorious, and I want to be used to point to Your glory. I ask for courage to say yes to You, in even the strangest things You ask of me. I ask for grace when I would rather run, and strength to teach my children the same. Amen.

Ponder:

1. How would our lives look different if we practiced first-time obedience to the Lord's leading?
2. What's one way you can obey God this week?

Take a Moment:

I've made this recipe for Eggnog Bread every Christmas for the past decade. It makes a bread that's not overly sweet, not too "noggy," and the top of the loaf gets caramelized and delicious. It makes a great breakfast treat, and goes perfectly with a hot cup of coffee.

EGGNOG BREAD

This loaf is one of my favorites to make as soon as eggnog hits the grocery shelves! It freezes nicely and makes a perfect gift for a neighbor or friend. Double the recipe and keep an extra loaf in the freezer – take it out to thaw in the morning before work, and it'll be ready for a perfect after-school snack! Makes one large loaf.

INGREDIENTS:

2 eggs
1 C. sugar
1 C. eggnog
½ C. butter, melted
1 tsp. vanilla
2 ¼ C. all-purpose flour
2 tsp. baking powder
¼ tsp. grated nutmeg

INSTRUCTIONS:

1. Preheat oven to 350°.
2. Beat eggs in a large mixing bowl.
3. Add sugar, eggnog, butter, and vanilla to eggs in bowl. Blend well, then set aside.
4. In a separate bowl, combine flour, baking powder, and nutmeg.
5. Add flour mixture to eggnog mixture and stir until just combined.
6. Pour into a greased 9×5" loaf pan.
7. Bake 65-70 minutes, or until wooden toothpick inserted in center comes out clean.

8. Remove pan from oven and place on wire rack. Cool for 10 minutes.
9. Carefully remove loaf from pan and let stand on wire rack until completely cool.
10. Slice and enjoy!

DECEMBER 19

"Look! I am sending my messenger, and he will prepare the way before me. Then the Lord you are seeking will suddenly come to his Temple. The messenger of the covenant, whom you look for so eagerly, is surely coming," says the LORD of Heaven's Armies.
MALACHI 3:1

Jesus came to Earth. Jesus came to pave the way for His Dad. Jesus came to show us God with skin on. Jesus, the messenger of God's promise delivered centuries before, came. And He will surely come again.

So, we rightfully celebrate – with twinkly lights, choirs singing, treats a-plenty, thoughtful gifts, family gatherings, and trees adorned. But right now, only mid-way through the month, we're not yet there yet. We're still anticipating the remembrance of Jesus' coming with seeking and eager hearts. Only days away, yet we're not quite ready.

I don't know about you but when I'm getting ready to celebrate, I clean. Often our celebrations are hosted in my home, so I spend hours vacuuming, dusting, scrubbing toilets, unloading and reloading the dishwasher, shoving the laundry behind a door that can close... you get the idea. I bet you do the same when you're expecting visitors (I hope I'm not the only one who cleans the most when company's coming!). I make lists and shop for groceries, I cook, and I serve. I get dressed, brush my teeth and hair, fix my lip gloss if it's a fancy gathering. I dress my kiddos and get them ready too, straightening their rooms and spaces, talking them through our plans and the roles they have and letting them know what to expect. I don't mind one bit of the getting ready; it's time to pray for my family and friends who will be coming over soon, it's time to give thanks for all we have, and it's time to shift my heart and make it ready for hosting.

I prepare myself, my home, and my family, and often I do it joyfully.

In what ways does your heart need preparation for Christmas? More quiet time to fill your heart, diving into the to-do list to clear space in your head, or making snow angels with your 5-year-old? What will settle your soul and fill it with joyful anticipation? And how about your house – what type of preparation does your house need? We're not talking a deep-clean, purge everything, kind of preparing, but how about a simple tidying and straightening up tonight?

What things truly need to be done in the few days left before Christmas to prepare the way for Him to enter your heart?

Think on your answers, make space for them in your schedule, and let the rest fall to the wayside. Let's be intentional about keeping our main priorities in the spotlighted center stage of our lives, and keep our hands open to release the rest.

Whether we're ready or not, Jesus is coming. Let's do the best we can to prepare, and then celebrate big.

Pray:

Lord, help me to keep my main things the main things. You, my family, and then the extras. May I keep the path to my heart cleared for You to easily enter in. Amen.

Ponder:

1. Are there unfinished projects on your list that are bothering you?
2. Can you finish them, or would you be okay to let them fall off the list?

Take a Moment:

Simple: only buy wrapping paper you really like, be it bright & shiny or brown paper. 'Tis the season of joy, friends, and that includes the littlest things. Why spend HOURS wrapping and staring at patterns that don't bring joy to our hearts?

I know. It's wrapping paper. Not a big deal. Actually, it's quite a small deal. But if we set a precedent of only bringing items that we treasure into our home, and if we start with the littlest of things, we'll start to build muscle memory. The idea of only using that which brings us joy can begin to shift our hearts and lead our actions in both big and small ways. So start with wrapping paper, then see where you go from there.

DECEMBER 20

John the Baptist, who was in prison, heard about all the things the Messiah was doing. So he sent his disciples to ask Jesus, "Are you the Messiah we've been expecting, or should we keep looking for someone else?"
MATTHEW 11:2-3

While he was in prison, John had his disciples ask Jesus the hard questions that he could not hold back, and we are welcomed to do the same.

Because God doesn't want our "fine." God wants our "real."

Sometimes Christmas is difficult, even amidst the wonderful, and we may not even know why. Our fears and sadness may rise to the surface and nothing we do can stop the flood of feelings. Amidst the bustle, the baking, the wrapping and the good cheer, I pray you let yourself feel whatever rises to the top of your heart this Christmas. Sadness, joy, guilt, exhaustion, nostalgia, a deep ache for those missing from our table.

Whatever the emotion, Christ came for its release.

His birth is our beginning too, and that precious Babe in the manger is big enough to lean into, weeping. As the carol sings, *"The hopes and fears of all the years are met in Thee tonight."* Every single one, met in Him.

May peace be yours, during this – the most wonderful and difficult time of the year.

Pray:

Lord, I have a lot of emotions this Christmas. In my feeling of them all, You are gracious and I am grateful. Help me to lean into You when I am overwhelmed, be it with sadness or joy -- in this season and all my seasons. Amen.

Ponder:

1. Spend some time giving space to hard feelings this season: memories, grief, whatever the struggle is.
2. Write in a journal, talk things over with a friend, pray deeply. Let yourself feel those emotions without adding guilt on top.

Take a Moment:

Load up the minivan and go for an evening drive! Whether by yourself or with the whole family, bring a thermos of hot tea or cocoa, crank the Christmas tunes, and set out to find local light displays.

CHRISTMAS REFLECTIONS

_____

_____

_____

_____

_____

_____

_____

_____

_____

_____

_____

_____

_____

_____

_____

_____

_____

DECEMBER 21

Wait patiently for the Lord. Be brave and courageous. Yes, wait patiently for the Lord.
PSALM 27:14

A couple of years ago, my husband and I stepped back after unloading the bins of Christmas decorations into our new-to-us townhome. We'd been married a couple of years and this was the first home we owned. We were so excited to make it our own, and to decorate it for the holidays!

After unpacking the bins of décor, we looked to admire our handiwork, and realized it looked like Christmas had "thrown up" in our house. There was no space in between one decorated area and another – every surface was covered!

We needed some open space for our beautiful decorations to be properly highlighted and enjoyed.

We went through the house and took down everything we didn't absolutely love. That helped. And each year since, if it's not meaningful to any of us and if we don't truly love it, it goes into an empty bin. We donate whatever is in that bin. Since that first house, the number of Christmas décor bins has decreased significantly, and we're left with just the items we adore.

It's a much more visually peaceful space to enter into now, with more breathing room than before.

In the same way that our first home needed more calm from the clutter, it's the empty space between the celebrations, the ornaments, and the special times that make them each able to shine. I've found that the emptiness – the quieted space – is called *peace*. And peace is a major part of Christmas.

Peace found its way to the first Christmas. The night began with a stressful and chaotic attempt to find a place to have a baby. Afterward, the contents of heaven were displayed in the most intense manner ever shown to earth, as angels filled the sky and sang in full belting chorus. And in between, The Baby was born. The birth itself was probably not peaceful, but in some of the moments following, there was quiet. There was peace.

Christ came in peace. He is for peace – in our hearts and in our lives, in both big and small ways.

Pray:

Lord, fill this heart, this home, this family, with peace -- the kind that only comes from You and that can be felt deeply, quietly, in the in-between. Help us to provide You with space this season, and to notice Your presence in it. Amen.

Ponder:

1. What's waiting for you this Christmas in the empty spaces, in the "in between" of your busy-ness?
2. Where are you finding peace?

Take a Moment:

Time for another quiet evening. Put away all the noise for a bit. Light a candle, turn on the Christmas tree lights, make a cup of hot chocolate and just soak in the peace (even if it's only five minutes before you're interrupted!)

Not only is it good for your soul to rest, it's good to model this kind of peaceful and restful behavior to our families.

DECEMBER 22

*No one lights a lamp and then covers it with a
bowl or hides it under a bed. A lamp is placed on a
stand, where its light can be seen by all who enter
the house. For all that is secret will eventually be
brought into the open, and everything that is
concealed will be brought to light and made
known to all.*
LUKE 8:16-17

Christmas is a perfect time to let our
lights shine in public. There are countless
volunteer opportunities, donation centers,
bells to ring, general goodwill and
merriment to spread. . . But what about the
chances we have to shine in our own homes?
To choose goodwill over frustration, to
volunteer instead of demand, to ring of joy
rather than discord?

Do you ever feel like it's easier to be a
better person to those outside our homes
than to the ones in it? I struggle with this.
Sometimes it's exhausting to shine, and
home is a place to rest.

Simply because we are in our real, messy,
everyday lives doesn't mean that we get to
conceal the light that God has placed in us. It
means we're called to shine it that much
brighter, and it's also that much harder to
do!

Home is where you can be your worst
self, yet still be loved. To shine at home as
you do in public can go against a regular
pattern of coming home and falling apart,

where it's safe to do so. While it will definitely be a challenge to shine within our own walls, it's one that comes with promise of growth for our whole families.

What if we considered our family members, co-workers, and anyone else we see on a regular basis a kind of "undercover angel"? Knowing that our behavior and attitude could be checked at any moment?

Because the truth is that choosing to let our light shine brightest right in our own homes will always be difficult, but it will also always be worth it.

Pray:

Lord, help the person I am at home match or even exceed the person I am in public. Give me strength when it would be so much easier to hide my light under the bed alongside the dust bunnies. Help me choose to place my lamp on a stand within my own home this season. Amen.

Ponder:

1. When is it most difficult for you to shine your light at home?
2. How can you intentionally struggle through that in order to shine brightly?

Take a Moment:

I discovered this recipe several years ago just days before my first child was born. Many years later now, and he's the first one in line to grab a handful. We've got the recipe down and this remains one of our family's favorites holiday season treats!

PEPPERMINT POPCORN CRUNCH

If you're feeling generous, you can put a scoop of this sweet and salty popcorn in a little bag, tie with a ribbon, and bring to a friend. But if you eat the whole batch yourself, there will be no judging from me. Makes about eight cups.

INGREDIENTS:
2 bags microwave popcorn*
1 12-oz. bag vanilla candy melts
¼ tsp. peppermint extract**
1 Tbs. vegetable oil
1-2 bag(s) peppermint M&M's™
Christmas sprinkles or sanding sugar

INSTRUCTIONS:
1. Pop the popcorn as directed.
2. Pour popped corn onto a rimmed cookie sheet. Remove as many un-popped kernels as possible, then pour popcorn into large bowl.
3. In separate glass bowl, melt the candy melts for 1 minute, then for 30-second intervals, stirring between each time until completely melted.
4. Stir vegetable oil and peppermint extract into the melted candy.
5. Pour candy melt mixture over the popcorn and mix together. It's messy but I've found that it works best to dig in with your hands and gently toss to mix!

6. Add the M&M's™ and gently mix (again, use your hands!)
7. Add sprinkles or sanding sugar before popcorn is fully cooled.
8. Once popcorn is fully cooled, store in an airtight container.

Notes:
*Substitute a large batch of stovetop or air-popped popcorn for the microwaved bags. If you do this, add 1 tbsp. melted butter and a few generous pinches of sea salt to the plain popped popcorn.

**Peppermint oil is a good alternative if you don't have peppermint extract on hand. If you use peppermint oil, add 2-3 drops.

DECEMBER 23

Look at my Servant, whom I have chosen. He is my Beloved, who pleases me. I will put my Spirit upon him, and he will proclaim justice to the nations. He will not fight or shout or raise his voice in public. He will not crush the weakest reed or put out a flickering candle. Finally, he will cause justice to be victorious. And his name will be the hope of all the world.
MATTHEW 12:18-21

Injustice seems bigger at Christmas. The needs of the world seem great, and our resources seem even smaller than usual. There are also many, many more ways to help than we see the rest of the year. People seem more driven to do good at the holidays. Is it because our hearts enlarge with hope during these holy days? Or are the injustices and our hearts always this big, but our vision clouded the rest of the year? Either way, we know that while we can't champion all the causes, we can make a difference to a few.

What cause makes your heart beat fast for people? Is it poverty in your hometown, human trafficking & slavery on a global scale, or water unclean to drink? Is it homelessness, abused & abandoned animals, or the environment? Whatever it is, if it's a big deal to you and your family, then it's important to pay attention to it and get plugged in to an organization that can help. Volunteering is a wonderful way to both spend time together as a family, do some honest good, and even spread Christmas cheer.

We can do this the rest of the year too. Goodwill isn't limited to the holidays. Get plugged in now, and let it propel you throughout the rest of winter.

Jesus came to bring justice, and He uses our hands to help.

Choose causes that resonate with your – and your family's – heart. Support those organizations this holiday season, and trust that while the needs are many and the resources few, Jesus has not forgotten that His name is hope.

Pray:
Lord, sometimes I feel small. In light of so many struggles, my offering seems meager. Will You make it bless? Will You take it and go all loaves and fishes on it, multiplying its worth? Most importantly, put in my heart a passion for the needs of Your people. Amen.

Ponder:
1. What makes your heart beat fast for people?
2. With that in mind, what is one cause or charitable organization you can give to this year, be it from your time, talents, or treasures?

Take a Moment:
In addition to the whole giving back/doing good aspect, the convenience of

donating online can't be beat. Most websites even provide a customizable printable for your recipient. Easy and impactful? Yes please! Here are a few of my favorite organizations to donate to at Christmas, and all year round:

- **World Vision**
  donate.worldvision.org
- **International Justice Mission**
  gifts.ijm.org
- **Heifer International**
  heifer.org
- **The Sheridan Story**
  thesheridanstory.org
  (This is local to Minnesota, but there are other similar organizations around the United States.)

DECEMBER 24:
CHRISTMAS EVE

So anyone who becomes as humble as this little child is the greatest in the Kingdom of Heaven.
MATTHEW 18:4

Is there any more wonder-filled day for kids than Christmas Eve? They're out of school (which is wonderful in and of itself), knowing two days of traditions are about to unfold, while presents beckon and stockings await filling. . . And many of them will lie awake long into the night listening for the peal of silvery sleigh bells.

Children are awe-filled at Christmas. Beyond any tired, tantrum, and cranky they can churn out, there is wonder. The simple sights and smells of the season charm their hearts, and their eyes are open to how extraordinary our ordinary days are.

Do you feel you've lost the "childlike" from your faith, longing to feel even a twinge of the glow you see in your children?

Making space for wonder is a choice, and it can be a difficult one for adults. After all, we're the realists, right? We know exactly how long we can stretch an hour and a dollar. We carry the details for each member of our family, keeping track of ALL THE THINGS and ALL THE LISTS. Adulting is hard and also our job, and there are times we do it well.

But no matter how great we are at managing details and tasks, we still need space and time for that which once made our faith childlike. We still need to let our hearts light up at a beautiful Christmas light display, a favorite carol coming on to the radio at just the right time, and a perfectly glittery snowfall. Notice the twinkly lights spreading warmth throughout home and heart. Fully enjoy the delicious foods and treats that come just once a year. Give thanks for the packages and cards arriving in the mail and under the tree.

If you're craving wonder, look no further than the eyes of your kids, and see the awe in the story of Jesus. May you bask in the glow that seems to spill from even the dustiest corners of your life, and may you allow wonder to fill your heart like a freshly fallen snow.

Pray:

Jesus, help me to be humble as a child, and to trust You with childlike faith. Thank you for the way You turn things upside-down in and for Your Kingdom, and thank You for this wondrous, ordinary, extraordinary day. Amen.

Ponder:

1. What keeps you from living "humble as a child"? Is it fear, pride, or something else?
2. Take time to identify what, if anything, gets in the way for your heart, then spend time in prayer asking God to remove it.

Take a Moment:

Get cozy and make some real-life-wonderful family memories. Surprise each family member with a gift to open - new jammies to wear tonight! Grab blankets & pillows and snuggle up in front of the Christmas tree. Read the Christmas story from a children's Bible, no matter how old your kids are. It will give the old, familiar, story new perspective.

DECEMBER 25:
CHRISTMAS DAY

At that time the Roman emperor, Augustus, decreed that a census should be taken throughout the Roman Empire. (This was the first census taken when Quirinius was governor of Syria.) All returned to their own ancestral towns to register for this census. And because Joseph was a descendant of King David, he had to go to Bethlehem in Judea, David's ancient home. He traveled there from the village of Nazareth in Galilee. He took with him Mary, his fiancée, who was now expecting a child. And while they were there, the time came for her baby to be born. She gave birth to her firstborn son. She wrapped him snugly in strips of cloth and laid him in a manger, because there was no lodging available for them.

That night there were shepherds staying in the fields nearby, guarding their flocks of sheep. Suddenly, an angel of the Lord appeared among them, and the radiance of the Lord's glory surrounded them. They were terrified, but the angel reassured them. "Don't be afraid!" he said. "I bring you good news that will bring great joy to all people. The Savior—yes, the Messiah, the Lord—has been born today in Bethlehem, the city of David! And you will recognize him by this sign: You will find a baby wrapped snugly in strips of cloth, lying in a manger." Suddenly, the angel was joined by a vast host of others—the armies of heaven—praising God and saying, "Glory to God in highest heaven, and peace on earth to those with whom God is pleased."

When the angels had returned to heaven, the shepherds said to each other, "Let's go to Bethlehem! Let's see this thing that has happened, which the Lord has told us about." They hurried to the village and found Mary and Joseph. And there was the baby, lying in the manger. After seeing him, the shepherds told everyone what had happened and what the angel had said to them about this child. All who heard the shepherds' story were astonished, but Mary kept all these things in her heart and thought about them often. The shepherds went back to their flocks, glorifying and praising God for all they had heard and seen. It was just as the angel had told them.
LUKE 2:1-20

You've worked and prepared, and now it's here. You've journeyed for four weeks, maybe more, but at least that long.

You've cleaned and scrubbed, shopped and wrapped, made memories and to-do lists.

You've baked and rested, gone to parties and chosen to stay at home, decorated and donated.

You've read stories and Scripture, taken photos and tied shoelaces, trimmed the tree and wiped the countertops.

The work is done. The day is here. Sister, you have done enough and now it is time to celebrate.

Merry Christmas, mama!

On this joyous and beloved day of days, truly be with your family. Put down the phone, the lists, the expectations, and just be with your people. Let go of any expectations of perfection that are still hanging around your heart, and embrace your real-life extraordinary. It's all your family really wants for Christmas.

It's all God wants for Christmas, too.

Pray:

Happy Birthday, Jesus! I am deeply grateful You came. Today we celebrate You, Jesus – Your birth and the life You lived. We love You. Amen.

Take a Moment:

Enjoy this day! Be silly, be love-filled, be present. Wear matching pajamas and eat too many cookies. Burn the candles down to the wick. Stay up late and go to church. Read a book and play with toys. Sing carols and laugh a lot.

Praise the God who came as a baby to save us all. Be together, give thanks, and have a Merry Christmas!

CHRISTMAS REFLECTIONS

_____

_____

_____

_____

_____

_____

_____

_____

_____

_____

_____

_____

_____

_____

_____

_____

PRAYERS FOR MOMS AT CHRISTMAS

These are prayers for you to whisper when you've hit a wall. When thinking of your own words is just too much, when you feel a bit bulldozed by the swiftness of the season, and when you need a real live silent night. When you're in that place, I invite you to pray the prayer you need (even if it feels silly) and know that I will be thinking of and praying for you during this blessed and busy Christmas season.

Prayer for the Parking Lot

Oh Lord. I know you have so, so, SO many more important things to hear and consider. I feel foolish even bringing this to You, yet You said I can talk to You about anything, so here I am. God, first I want to find a parking spot. One that is close to the front door of the store and big enough for my minivan. Then, I'd like my kids to stay near me (instead of running into traffic) as we navigate the parking lot and meander into the store. Finally, when we leave, I'd love to be able to find my car – even if I have to use the panic button on my keychain to make the car honk.

Like I said, I know how this sounds. But Lord, I'm asking for grace today. I need some so I can give some. Thanks, God. Amen.

Prayer for Just One Perfect Place

Lord, if one more kid, or my husband, or even the cat pokes around underneath the tree again, so help me I'll throw all the gifts into the garage. I thought it was pretty good to have everything wrapped already, and maybe I was asking for it by arranging them all nicely under the branches. But Lord, I just wanted one place in the house that looks close to perfect. I know that's not a very noble goal, but can't I just have one place?

Give me patience, God – I know my family is just so excited they can't even stand it. And honestly, I am too. I love Your birthday, Jesus. But. Keep the cat out of the tree? Thanks, Lord. Amen.

Prayer for Family Christmas Dinner

OK. Here we go. We've been cooking and/or driving all day to get to this dinner. Would you pull some kind of miracle, God? Help my kids to remember the manners I've tried so hard to instill. Could You make sure that they don't declare the yams "icky," slosh water across the table, or crack the china? Create space in the hearts of the other guests for my kids to be kids. Help our extended family to realize how sweet and dear my kiddos are, even as they're carefully arranging the food on their plate into color piles.

Help me to breathe it all in deeply, this beautiful mess of family all gathered at one table? There are people we miss dearly who aren't sitting with us this year – may we allow ourselves to feel that ache, and to be grateful for the ones who are here in the chairs.

We gather in Your name, Jesus. Amen.

Prayer for Christmas Eve

It's here, Lord -- my favorite night of the whole year. Not many other nights promise the peace and joy that this one does, and you know, it almost always delivers. Sure, I'll be up wrestling with toy packaging and forgetting to stuff the stockings. And there's no point in setting the alarm because those currently dreaming kids of ours will run into our room at the crack of dawn.

But as my husband and I catch each other's eye across a mountain of discarded plastic and wrapping paper bits, we'll revel in the wonderous gift it is to get to love our family, and that You understand every bit of that love.

Thank you for sending Your Son to be born. Thank you for beginning His magnificent life with such an unassuming entrance. His birth sets the tone for our faith – walk humbly, love mercy, seek justice. All done in one night in Bethlehem. Grant me just one moment of quiet peace in front of the tree tonight?

Thank you for coming for me, Jesus. I adore you. Amen.

Prayer for Christmas Morning

Happy birthday, Jesus!

Good grief, it's here already! That was a very short night. I am so, so grateful You were born, Lord.

Would You send me some extraordinary energy today? Because the kids who just threw themselves on our bed need me to be able to keep up with their joy today, and I really want to, but I need Your help.

Thank You for being joy, and for sending some extra on this day of days. Please send coffee and peace next.

Thank You for coming, Jesus. We're going to celebrate You big today.

Prayer for the New Year

There are so many hopes and dreams laid on this one day, Lord – so many people relying on its passing to bring a clean slate. And then in two days when resolutions are already dashed, disappointment rears up ugly and defeating.

God, You promise to provide new beginnings and new mercies each morning as they dawn, fresh and unspoiled. Thank you for that.

As we enter a new year, I ask You to stay at the forefront of our days, that we may claim those new beginnings and mercies, and that this would be a blessed year. We know it will be because You are already there. Thank You, Lord. Amen.

ACKNOWLEDGEMENTS

This book would not exist without the love and support from a village-full. I'll never be able to adequately thank them for believing in me and my words, and for giving me the time needed to think and type them out.

My husband Jared: thank you for so fiercely believing in my words, even and especially when they wouldn't come to mind. You're the gale force wind to my breeze. For your patience, wisdom, entrepreneurial spirit, and digital know-how. . . this absolutely would not have happened without you and your gifts. Thanks for making space for me to write this book. Love you.

Sam, Josie, and Clara: thank you for watching the *Berenstain Bears* and *Daniel Tiger* while Mommy wrote. Thank you for cheering for me – my favorite writing happened after your choruses of, "Go mommy go! You can do it!" I can do it, because of your love. Thank you for being the BEST kids in the whole world. I love you so much!

My mom (best known as Mormor): we took over your house by storm while I wrote and packaged and shipped this book, and I think you're still picking up the proverbial (and actual) pieces from that season. Thank you for continuing to make space for us, and for watching my children so I could crank out a few pages at a time. Thank you for being the safe place to all of your kids and grandkids. You are so loved.

My (in)courage team: Joy Groblebe, Grace P. Cho, and Becky Keife –working and writing alongside you is an honor and joy, as it is to work with a team who "gets it," who understands all of it – the writing, the working from home, and the mothering. As far as I'm concerned, we're pretty much the dream team. Everyone stay in your seats on the bus.

My best ones: Kayse Pratt, Mary Carver, Kristin Taylor, Erika Dawson, Amanda Conquers, and Christen Price – you are a straight up gift. Thank you for the advice and words of wisdom, the ideas and conversations, the affirmation and encouragement. You are my favorites and I am so thankful for you!

To the One who is Immanuel, who was born into a broken world to break Himself and redeem our hearts. You are the reason for much more than just this season. You are everything. All I have is Yours. Happy Birthday.

Merry Christmas!

Anna E. Rendell

ABOUT THE AUTHOR

Anna E. Rendell is the author of several devotionals for women, including *Pumpkin Spice for Your Soul* and *A Moment of Christmas*. She is the Digital Content Manager at (in)courage by DaySpring, an online writer and a speaker, sharing encouragement with moms and women. She lives in Minnesota with her husband and their three kids, who provide plenty of fodder for her #realmomconfessions online. Anna loves a good book and a great latte.

For more from Anna, visit AnnaRendell.com, and find her on all social media at @annaerendell.

MORE BOOKS BY ANNA E. RENDELL

Pumpkin Spice for Your Soul: 25 Devotions for Autumn

The season of autumn is both beloved and brief. In *Pumpkin Spice for Your Soul*, Anna Rendell encourages you to drink deep and savor this favorite time of year. Each of the 25 days in this book includes a Scripture verse, devotion, question to ponder, and an "extra shot" – a recipe, inspiring quote, or fun autumn idea – like espresso for your soul! Anna's writing is to-the-point, encouraging and lighthearted. She will help you fully experience and take delight in pumpkin spice season!

A Moment of Quiet: 25 Two-Minute Prayers for Moms

Each prayer in this e-book is written in the first person so that you may simply sit, breathe, and pray as needed. Pull up a prayer on your phone while you're hiding in the bathroom. Whisper one between laundry cycles. Say another out loud while you're parked in the driveway, not yet ready to go inside. Say a prayer for yourself, and whisper one on behalf of another mother who could use even a moment of quiet.

Find these books at annarendell.com/mybooks.

Made in United States
Troutdale, OR
11/27/2024